CAROL ANN DUFFY: THE PAMPHLET

By Carol Ann Duffy

Standing Female Nude

Selling Manhattan

The Other Country

Mean Time

Carol Ann Duffy: The Pamphlet

ANVIL PRESS POETRY

Published in 1998
by Anvil Press Poetry Ltd
Neptune House 70 Royal Hill London SE10 8RF

This book is published with financial assistance
from The Arts Council of England

Designed and set in Monotype Janson by Anvil
Printed and bound in England
by Redwood Books Trowbridge Wiltshire

ISBN 0 85646 307 8

A catalogue record for this book
is available from the British Library

For Jackie with love

ACKNOWLEDGEMENTS

Acknowledgements are due to the Museum of Scotland who commissioned 'Standing Stone', and to BBC Radio, the *Independent* and the *Times Literary Supplement* where other poems first appeared.

CONTENTS

Standing Stone

Commissioned for the opening of The Museum of Scotland, 30 November 1998

I

Who carved a bird and a fish
on a standing stone?
What kind of a fish?
An Alec, a Bream, a Burt, a Char,
a Cunner, a Cusk, a Dab, a Dace, a Drumfish
that swam in the Dee, the Don, the Spey,
the Tay, the Forth, the Annan, the Nith,
the Clyde and the Tweed
before these rivers were words –
before the bird was a word,
though your finger tracing its shape
in the stone
knows it's a géadh, a goose.

Before History starts, a skein of geese fly,
like an arrow into the present tense,
over Callanish.
What lies in the soil?
An arrowhead made of flint
holding its tongue.
A bowl of bronze begging for light.
A bangle. A brooch. A bonnet-piece.
A dirk. A lunula.
A shield, grooved and scratched like an old LP.
Wheesht.
Listen.
Who's that clagging his spade on a shield
as he digs a grave for a dog?

2

I was digging a hole
for the deid dug,
when a dull clank
had me up tae ma oxters in mud
and I pulls oot this shield.

I held it up tae the light
like a winner, somebody famous;
and I kenned it was worth a few quid,
pure bronze under the cowpats and dirt.
Then I ran like a warrior
over the loaning,
banging the shield with ma fist,
calling and calling the name of ma wife –
till she stood at the door tae the byre
in the gloamin,
held in the amber light of the sun
like a girl frae the Bronze Age.

3

Inside History now,
a woman stands near a byre
dipping the crystal healing-charm of her clan
into the cattle-trough.
She kens this will cure the cows
sick in the loaning.
She kens that a calf's heart
stuck through with pins
will guard against evil.

Inside History now,
a woman stoops at the edge
of Kilbirnie Loch
and scoops water for washing the hands
into a ewer,
which slips from her living grasp
and gargles away
into the loch
for five hundred years.
Now what did they cry her?

And what did they cry her
with the glamorous eyes
and the red hair
who was hauled up in front of the outraged men
of the Kirk
and punished well
for her godless, lascivious, hellbent, adulterous
    ways –

Ye will be made to sit
in Greyfriars Church
throughout the Service,
clad in a goon of repentance
and sat on the stool of repentance
for all to see. Whooer.

And what is her body
thinking of
under yon sackcloth?

Of Davy MacLachlan, perhaps,
an Edinburgh Pewterer
known to her through her lawful spouse,

who slowly poured strong drink
from a tappit hen to a quaich,
drank it, then kissed it into her throat,
till she felt the ache
she is feeling now,
crouched on her punishment stool,
not knowing his kiss shines on her brazen face
under the thunderous gaze of the Kirk.

4

Davy MacLachlan stamped his mark
on the Touchplate, to guarantee
his good and faithful work, like a kiss;
slung his coat over his shooder
and whistled away into the New,
whistled away into the New.
Light and thought and grace were suddenly stone
in Princes Street, in Queen Street, in
    Charlotte Square.
His faither had cried it the Swamp,
the Nor' Loch – George Street, Hanover Street –
and had lost a sixpence, a bawbee, there
when he was a wean.
But Davy jingles British coins
in his breeks,
like it or no, right or wrong.
See that Act of Union, son?
There was an end to an auld sang.
Davy MacLachlan crosses the street.
He spies the glint of a copper coin
at his feet.

5

This is the bawbee of Kenneth MacLachlan,
didnae he bawl when it plopped in the swamp.
These are the guns of the Lairds of Grant,
the lugs are dust that heard them bang.
Here's the keys of Deacon Brodie,
wasnae he a respectable man.
This is the mask and the wig of Peden,
where are the eyes and the preaching tongue?
This is Betty Plenderloath's sampler,
Unto No Image Bow Thy Knee.
Here's a pound from the Union Bank of
    Scotland,
to fill six stockings on Christmas Eve.
Here's a thumbscrew, a heart-brooch,
    a hair-ring,
to torture, to charm, to mourn the deid.
Here's an ivory chessman from Lewis,
just who was in check as the seagulls jeered?
As the clouds of history swelled like sails
on the sea of the sky over Strathnaver,
as the ravens screamed in the Strath of Kildonan

and the centuries rolled over Inverness,
over Peterhead, Iona, Perth, over Edinburgh,
Glasgow, Firth of Clyde. Come away inside
and look at this Pictish stone
carved with a goose and a fish.
Now who carved a bird and a fish
on a standing stone?

Three Swift Poems

I *My Favourite Drink*

was in The Red Dragon
in Penderyn
near Hirwaun
in mid-Glamorgan
where I ordered up
two halves
of Dark Brains
and took them out
to drink on the grass
alone
as a whopping apricot moon
bulged in the sky.

Remembering this
in words not dissimilar to these,
I count myself lucky indeed;
as I do
that you love me still
and the end of us both
is a good few years away yet.
Cheers.

2 *How*

Why don't I stand up and tell
the rest of the class
how I have ruined my life;
how my marriage
howled like a dog
on its chain,
how I left it too late
to forgive them,
my mother,
my father,
only human,
human as they were,
the haemorrhage of years;
how I wasted away
in a job,
travelling home
on the stopping train,
a woman who never found
her city or town,
her particular place;

how I purchased a flat
in a big old house
and watered my indoor plants,
how I wear one ring
with a cold blue stone
like an English eye;
and how,
to earn the approval of Helen Maguire,
pretty, spiteful Helen Maguire
who was not as clever as me,
I knelt at her feet
in the playground
and licked, as she told me to do,
the dust
from her brown school shoes,
the dust from her shoes.

3 *Lost Weather*

How does an astronaut feel
who went to the moon
should he chance to look up
one night on his own
to see the startling light of his past
where he took
his one small step
for a man.

Tonight on my own
on the tip of my tongue
the taste of a snowflake
refuses to yield
lost weather, the patterns
my mother made
before my eyes
in the beautiful hurting light of the snow.

A Disbelief

This is myself outside in the rain.
I can't speak our language. The locks
have been changed. The worst
that can possibly happen will.

The worst that can possibly happen
will. The flowers I planted
drown in weeds. You pull the curtains
against the night. But this is myself

circling the house, counting the lights
in precious rooms. What do you say
behind the glass? A lamp goes out.
Despair. A damp and heavy coat.

Love is a form of prayer; love lost
a disbelief. No words from the faithless dark
can mean. I had the key once,
opened the front door, calling your name.

Because I knew, I dreamt for years
the worst that can possibly happen will
and everything good run into a drain.
This is myself outside in the rain.

Holloway Road

Penelope, when my tube-train stops
at Holloway Road
I remember when you
were minutes away,
a head-down rush
with a bottle of red
in a brown paper bag
through London rain
to your house which never, so long as I live,
will I visit again;

and remember as well
how you'd open the door
with your head to one side
as though a joke
were half-way told
and the sight of a friend
was the punchline itself.
So you'd laugh them in,
whoever they were,

through to the kitchen.
Never again will I follow you down the hall
 there.

Or, Penelope, if I got out here,
as I sometimes did,
and took a cab
down Holloway Road,
a turn to the left
then a swing to the third on the right
won't bring me face
to your living face
before you were ill
and couldn't get well
and died
with no warning or reason at all.

I lose you again
behind sliding doors
in the moment it takes
for the night-shift driver
to ease the brakes,
pulling away from Holloway Road,

Piccadilly Line,
Penelope,
into the dark.
The tunnel is long.
On I go
towards Arsenal, Finsbury Park.

Circe

I'm fond, nereids and nymphs, unlike some, of
    the pig,
of the tusker, the snout, the boar and the swine.
One way or another, all pigs have been mine –
under my thumb, the bristling, salty skin of
    their backs,
in my nostrils here, their yobby, porky colognes.
I'm familiar with hogs and runts, their
    percussion of oinks
and grunts, their squeals. I've stood with a pail
    of swill
at dusk, at the creaky gate of the sty,
tasting the sweaty, spicy air; the moon
like a lemon popped in the mouth of the sky.
But I want to begin with a recipe from abroad

which uses the cheek – and the tongue in cheek
at that. Lay two pig's cheeks, with the tongue,
in a dish, and strew it well over with salt
and cloves. Remember the skills of the tongue –
to lick, to lap, to loosen, lubricate, to lie
in the soft pouch of the face – and how each
    pig's face
was uniquely itself, as many handsome as plain,
the cowardly face, the brave, the comical, noble,
sly or wise, the cruel, the kind, but all of them,
nymphs, with those piggy eyes. Season with
    mace.

Well-cleaned pigs' ears should be blanched,
singed, tossed
in a pot, boiled, kept hot, scraped, served, garnished
with thyme. Look at that simmering lug, at that ear,
did it listen, ever, to you, to your prayers and
rhymes,
to the chimes of your voice, singing and clear? Mash
the potatoes, nymph, open the beer. Now to the
brains,
to the trotters, shoulders, chops, to the sweet
meats slipped
from the slit, bulging, vulnerable bag of the balls.
When the heart of a pig has hardened, dice it small.

Dice it small. I, too, once knelt on this shining
    shore
watching the tall ships sail from the burning sun
like myths; slipped off my dress to wade,
breast-deep, in the sea, waving and calling;
then plunged, then swam on my back,
    looking up
as three black ships sighed in the shallow waves.
Of course, I was younger then. And hoping for
    men. Now,
let us baste that sizzling pig on the spit once
    again.

Mrs Faust

First things first –
I married Faust.
We met as students,
shacked up, split up,
made up, hitched up,
got a mortgage on a house,
flourished academically,
BA. MA. PhD. No kids.
Two towelled bathrobes. Hers. His.

We worked. We saved.
We moved again.
Fast cars. A boat with sails.
A second home in Wales.
The latest toys – computers,
mobile phones. Prospered.
Moved again. Faust's face
was clever, greedy, slightly mad.
I was as bad.

I grew to love the lifestyle,
not the life.
He grew to love the kudos,
not the wife.
He went to whores.
I felt, not jealousy,
but chronic irritation.
I went to yoga, tai chi,
Feng Shui, therapy, colonic irrigation.

And Faust would boast
at dinner parties
of the cost
of doing deals out East.
Then take his lust
to Soho in a cab,
to say the least,
to lay the ghost,
get lost, meet panthers, feast.

He wanted more.
I came home late one winter's evening,
hadn't eaten.

Faust was upstairs in his study,
in a meeting.
I smelled cigar smoke,
hellish, oddly sexy, not allowed.
I heard Faust and the other
laugh aloud.

Next thing, the world,
as Faust said,
spread its legs.
First Politics –
Safe seat. MP. Right Hon. KG.
Then banks –
offshore, abroad –
and business –
Vice-chairman. Chairman. Owner. Lord.

Enough? *Encore!*
Faust was Cardinal, Pope,
knew more than God;
flew faster than the speed of sound
around the globe,
lunched;

walked on the moon,
golfed, holed in one;
lit a fat Havana on the sun.

Then backed a hunch –
invested in smart bombs,
in harms,
Faust dealed in arms.
Faust got in deep, got out.
Bought farms,
cloned sheep,
Faust surfed the Internet
for like-minded Bo-Peep.

As for me,
I went my own sweet way,
saw Rome in a day,
spun gold from hay,
had a face-lift,
had my breasts enlarged,
my buttocks tightened;
went to China, Thailand, Africa,
returned, enlightened.

Turned 40, celibate,
teetotal, vegan,
Buddhist, 41.
Went blonde,
redhead, brunette,
went native, ape,
berserk, bananas;
went on the run, alone;
went home.

Faust was in. *A word*, he said,
I spent the night being pleasured
by a virtual Helen of Troy.
Face that launched a thousand ships.
I kissed its lips.
Thing is –
I've made a pact
with Mephistopheles,
the Devil's boy.

He's on his way
to take away
what's owed,

reap what I sowed.
For all these years of
gagging for it,
going for it,
rolling in it,
I've sold my soul.

At this, I heard
a serpent's hiss,
tasted evil, knew its smell,
as scaly devil hands
poked up
right through the terracotta Tuscan tiles
at Faust's bare feet
and dragged him, oddly smirking, there and then
straight down to Hell.

Oh, well.
Faust's will
left everything –
the yacht,
the several homes,
the Lear jet, the helipad,

the loot, et cet, et cet,
the lot –
to me.

C'est la vie.
When I got ill,
it hurt like hell.
I bought a kidney
with my credit card,
then I got well.
I keep Faust's secret still –
the clever, cunning, callous bastard
didn't have a soul to sell.

Mrs Icarus

I'm not the first or the last
to stand on a hillock,
watching the man she married
prove to the world
he's a total, utter, absolute, Grade A pillock.

Queens

A cold, bored Queen lived in a castle.
She was Queen as far as the castle walls,
    no farther.
Rooks flapped about. HM stared out from the
    East tower
in her blue robes, in the dull old gold of her
    crown;
a thin white Queen with grey-green eyes under
    a tight frown.

She wrote to a second Queen; she penned
    a formal letter
with a clammy candlewax seal. *I hope*
you are feeling better. Please come.
For three days, a man on a black horse
rode uphill with the letter.
For two days he rode downhill with the answer.
Very well. Very well.
A trembling royal hand reached out, tugged
at the hanging rope of the servants' bell.

Queen Two was fat, with a loud voice
and a temper.
She dressed in a piccalilli yellow.
Queen One came down to greet her
in the Great Pink Hall for dinner.
Clear soup. Spinach. Fish.
What's this? the big Queen bellowed,
Rubbish to make me thinner?
Where is the curry, the pepper, the pickle,
the onion, the mustard and chilli?
Where is the garlic bread?
I'm off to bed.

At daybreak, a quiet Queen sat by her chessboard,
pale, apprehensive, fainter of heart.
A cross Queen thumped in, unthin.
What's going on? Where are the boxing-gloves,
the duelling swords, the snooker cues, where are the
darts?
The rooks outside were alarmed, cawed back
at her deafening shout –
I'M GOING OUT!

That night, Queen One mooted a walk
in the castle grounds.
It was mild. There was a moon up above
and a moon in the moat.
They could stroll, calm, polite, Queen hand in
    Queen glove,
under the yews, the ancient oaks.
Is this a joke? Queen Two snapped.
Where are the bagpipes, the fiddlers three,
where is the karaoke? Answer me that!
TAXI!

So both Queens tried harder, harder.
Queen Thin let Queen Fat
raid the royal larder.
Fat held Thin's wool,
her big, plump, soft, regal hands
frozen mid-clap.
Queen Thin knitted away, click, click-clack,
    click-clack.
Then both Queens sat in a marble bath –
Fat at the bottom, Thin by the taps –
We are clean Queens, they sang,

We are fragrant.
We are very very very clean Queens.

And when it was time,
Queen One managed a slight bow of the head,
Queen Two shuffled the start of a curtsy
under her dress.
Farewell, farewell,
a fat Queen called from a gold coach,
trotting away down the gravel drive, over the
moat,
a big puce Queen
with a string of rubies at her throat.
Goodbye, goodbye.

Goodbye. A thin Queen waved from a window,
shyly,
then fingered her new pearls.
One two three four five six seven.
Seven rooks round a castle started to cry.

The Invention of Rain

Rain first came
when the woman whose lovely face
was the sky
cried.

She thought of rain
for her sadness,
her sorrowful clouds.
The woman whose lonely voice
was the wind
howled.

Then garden flowers
bowed their heads
under the bitter-sweet grief of the rain.

And an only child
stared down at them
through the thousand tears
of a window-pane.

To the Unknown Lover

Horrifying, the very thought of you,
whoever you are,
future knife to my scar,
stay where you are.

Be handsome, beautiful, drop-dead
gorgeous, keep away.
Read my lips.
No way. OK?

This old heart of mine's
a battered purse.
These ears are closed.
Don't phone, want dinner,

make things worse.
Your little quirks?
Your wee endearing ways?
What makes you you, all that?

Stuff it, mount it, hang it
on the wall, sell tickets,
I won't come. Get back. Get lost.
Get real. Get a life. Keep shtum.

And just, you must, remember this —
there'll be no kiss, no clinch,
no smoochy dance, no true romance.
You are *Anonymous.* You're *Who?*

Here's not looking, kid, at you.

Books by Carol Ann Duffy from Anvil Press Poetry

STANDING FEMALE NUDE

'Carol Ann Duffy is a very pure poet... It is good to see a crusading sensibility refusing to surrender any touch of art to the urgency of its cause'
– Peter Porter, *The Observer*

SELLING MANHATTAN

'*Selling Manhattan* is one of those rare books that is immediately enjoyable yet will repay many re-readings. Buy it'
– Vernon Scannell, *Poetry Review*

THE OTHER COUNTRY

'It voices political-erotic challenge, always knows where it's going, and has serious fun on the way'
– Ruth Padel, *The Times Literary Supplement*

MEAN TIME

'Carol Ann Duffy is one of the freshest and bravest talents to emerge in British poetry – any poetry – for years ... With her gift for risk and her no-nonsense music, she has more chance than most to write those poems which run what Frost called "a lucky course of events"'
– Eavan Boland, *The Independent on Sunday*

Mean Time received the Forward Poetry Prize and the Whitbread Poetry Award for 1993.